RIGHT
WHALES

This book is dedicated to Scott Kraus,
in whom right whales have their greatest champion;
and to Lindy Johnson, who as a tireless advocate for
the marine environment is a heroine to us all.

Text © 2004 by Phil Clapham

Printed in China

04 05 06 07 08 5 4 3 2 1

Library of Congress Cataloging-in-Publication Data

Clapham, Phil.
Right whales : natural history & conservation / Phil Clapham.
p. cm. — (WorldLife Library)
ISBN 0-89658-657-X (pbk. : alk. paper)
1. Right whales—Juvenile literature. I. Title. II. World life library.
QL737.C423C59 2004
599.5'2—dc22
2004014318

Distributed in Canada by Raincoast Books, 9050 Shaughnessy Street, Vancouver, B.C. V6P 6E5

Published by Voyageur Press, Inc.
123 North Second Street, P.O. Box 338, Stillwater, MN 55082 U.S.A.
651-430-2210, fax 651-430-2211
books@voyageurpress.com
www.voyageurpress.com

Educators, fundraisers, premium and gift buyers, publicists, and marketing managers:
Looking for creative products and new sales ideas? Voyageur Press books are available at special discounts when purchased in quantities, and special editions can be created to your specifications. For details contact the marketing department at 800-888-9653.

Photographs © 2004 by

Front cover © François Gohier
Back cover © François Gohier
Page 1 © Tom Walmsley/naturepl.com
Page 3 © Roland Seitre/Still Pictures
Page 4 © Jacqueline Russell
Page 6 © François Gohier
Page 9 © François Gohier
Page 10 © Jeff Foott/naturepl.com
Page 13 © Gabriel Rojo/naturepl.com
Page 15 © François Gohier
Page 16 © Doug Allan/Oxford Scientific Films
Page 19 © François Gohier
Page 20 © Armin Maywald/naturepl.com

Page 23 © François Gohier
Page 24 © François Gohier
Page 27 © Gabriel Rojo/naturepl.com
Page 28 © Doug Allan/Oxford Scientific Films
Page 31 © François Gohier
Page 32 © François Gohier
Page 35 © François Gohier
Page 36 © Tom Walmsley/naturepl.com
Page 39 © Tom Walmsley/naturepl.com
Page 40 © Jen & Des Bartlett
   Oxford Scientific Films
Page 43 © François Gohier
Page 44 © François Gohier

Page 47 © François Gohier
Page 48 © François Gohier
Page 51 © Jacqueline Russell
Page 52 © Jacqueline Russell
Page 55 © François Gohier
Page 56 © François Gohier
Page 59 © Gabriel Rojo/naturepl.com
Page 60 © François Gohier
Page 62 © François Gohier
Page 64 © François Gohier
Page 67 © François Gohier
Page 69 © François Gohier

RIGHT
WHALES

Phil Clapham

WORLDLIFE
LIBRARY

Voyageur Press

A right whale mother and her calf rest in calm waters. As is the case here, right whales can often be found very close to shore.

Contents

Right Whales   7

Origins   11

'True Whale of the Ice'   17

Individuals   25

Feeding: And the Largest Shall Prey Upon the Smallest   33

Reproduction, Behavior and Social Structure   41

The Right Whale to Kill   49

Conservation and the Future   57

Right Whales Distribution map   70

Right Whale Facts / Recommended Reading   71

Index / Biographical Note   72

Right Whales

We saw daily great whales, of the best kind for oil and bone, come close aboard and play about the ship. (Journal of the Mayflower Pilgrims)

It is November 1620. Inside the hook of Cape Cod, Massachusetts, in a place that will later come to be called Provincetown, a ship lies at anchor. Her name is *Mayflower*. She is a lowly cargo ship, a small, cramped and rather dumpy-looking vessel of distinctly unremarkable lines; yet she is destined to become one of the most famous ships in history. Aboard her, 100 passengers have just completed a 66-day voyage across the North Atlantic Ocean from England, a miserable journey marked by sea-sickness and storms, illness and death.

The passengers – Pilgrims seeking religious freedom and independence in the New World – crowd the rail to see what can be seen. Their eyes are no longer turned towards the ocean; after so many weeks of unbroken gray vistas of sea and sky, most of them have had enough of that vast and lonely realm to last a lifetime. Instead, they survey the unfamiliar but welcome landscape of their new home.

But suddenly, a strange sound causes them to return their gaze to the water. Amazed, they see a whale surface close by, its blow exploding from its body with a loud *whoosh*. The whale is black, with a smooth back and strange callous-like growths about its head. As it breathes, a spout emerges from the animal's great nostrils in a distinct V shape. And when the whale dives, it raises a huge black triangular tail high into the air.

Perhaps the sight of this monster of the deep frightens some of the Pilgrims, newly freed as they are from the sea's dangers. But at least one man aboard recognizes it as a right whale – an immensely valuable animal – and runs below decks to fetch his gun. A few moments later, the whale resurfaces even closer to the boat.

Excited, the man raises the old, rusty weapon, takes aim, fires – and is knocked off his feet, injured, as the gun explodes. Unconcerned, the whale swims away. In this first recorded encounter between whales and the new colonists, the anonymous right whale emerged in far better shape than its human adversary. But the interaction was an omen of things to come, the beginning of a long and sad history that would see humans multiply and right whales diminish in the waters of New England and elsewhere.

'The best kind for oil and bone...' For almost a thousand years, right whales were hunted by humans for the fine oil that could be rendered from their thick blubber, and for the long plates of baleen (referred to by whalers as *whalebone*, or simply *bone*) that, before the invention of plastic, were widely used in products ranging from corset stays to umbrella slats. Without exception, no species of great whale was persecuted for so long and so intensely as the right whale, and this unhappy legacy has left us with an animal that is on the brink of extinction in two of the three oceans which it inhabits.

In this book, I would like to introduce you to right whales. They are strange creatures in many ways – not sleek like the mighty blue whale, nor fast like the finback – yet they are extraordinary animals whose life history, feeding habits and mating system are truly fascinating. Hunted until well into the 20th century, right whales in many ways symbolize the reckless greed of the whaling industry. Today, while one of the three species of right whale is recovering well from these excesses, the two others – in the North Pacific and North Atlantic – are clearly not. Plagued by low numbers, fishing gear entanglements, ship collisions and other problems, their survival in the modern world is far from assured.

The Pilgrims who first encountered right whales in 1620 later commented that they were so abundant in the area that '*a man could almost walk across Cape Cod Bay upon their backs*'. Today, right whales are among the rarest of all mammals, and they are one of the top priorities for those charged with the conservation of the world's whales.

Origins

Scientists don't know for certain how long right whales have been plying the world's oceans, but we do know that they have been around a great deal longer than modern humans. The first animals that look like right whales appear in the fossil record some 20 million years ago. However, given that this record is notoriously incomplete, it's possible that right whales have existed for longer than this; and we do not know if these early fossils were the species that we know today, or an ancestral form.

Right whales are marine mammals which, like their mammalian counterparts on land, breathe air, give birth to live young, and nurse those young with milk. They are members of a group (the scientific term is an 'order') called cetaceans; the word cetacean derives from the Greek word *ketos,* meaning whale or sea monster. The cetaceans include all of the whales, dolphins and porpoises; the group encompasses animals that range in size from the tiny vaquita (less than 5 feet, or 1.5 m) to the mighty blue whale (adult females of which can exceed 100 feet or 30 m in length, and weigh more than 150 tons). In all, there are something like 80 species of cetaceans worldwide.

We say 'something like 80' because the exact number is in dispute. Some animals that are currently lumped under a single species name are in reality probably two or more separate species (right whales were until recently a good example of this; see below). It is also possible – as incredible as it may seem in this day and age – that not all species of cetaceans have been discovered. A new species of cetacean (called Perrin's beaked whale) was described as recently as 2002. In the same year another species whose existence was known only from two skulls (Longman's beaked whale) was observed in the wild for the first time. Remarkably, the oceans still hold secrets.

The origin of cetaceans can ultimately be traced to a time about 60 million years ago, when a group of mammals known as condylarths lived by the water. Condylarths were rather small animals that would become the ancestors not only of cetaceans, but also of the group of modern land mammals known as ungulates. Indeed, recent genetic analysis has suggested that the closest relative to cetaceans on land today is the hippopotamus.

The condylarths lived on coasts or in river estuaries at the edge of the Tethys Sea, an ancient body of water that covered much of what is now central Asia (the Mediterranean Sea is its last vestige). For whatever reason, this ancestral species began to spend time in the water, perhaps to escape predation or to exploit a new source of food there. While this move into an aquatic environment must have been advantageous, it presented the animals with many challenges. As a result, many adaptations began to occur in the animals' morphology and physiology, some of which we can see today in transitional fossils. Over millions of years, the body took on a more streamlined shape and developed a powerful horizontal tail for easier movement through the water. The hind limbs eventually disappeared, while the forelimbs were modified into flippers. The nose gradually moved back from the tip of the animal's snout to the top of its head, making it easier to breathe without water entering the lungs. Fat layers were thickened to give insulation in cold water. The animals also evolved the ability to dive for prolonged periods.

The earliest fossils of what are clearly true cetaceans – that is, completely aquatic mammals – appear approximately 45-50 million years ago. These are known as archaeocetes (the word means 'ancient whales'), and they included a considerable diversity of species. While none seem to have been the size of the huge blue or fin whales that we know today, some reached considerable lengths. For example, an archaeocete known as *Basilosaurus* was more than 70 feet (21 meters) long.

For some reason, the archaeocetes became extinct about 25-30 million years ago. However, by that time other lineages of cetaceans had begun to develop from the archaeocete stock, leading to the two groups (or 'suborders') of cetaceans that we see today. One of these groups, the odontocetes (from the Latin, meaning 'toothed whales') today comprise the majority of species, including all of the dolphins and porpoises as well as the sperm whale and a rather strange group known as the beaked whales. As the name indicates, all of the odontocetes have teeth, although the number varies by species from one to many.

By contrast, members of the other suborder have no teeth at all. These are the mysticetes (also a Latin word, meaning 'moustached whales')

A right whale leaps from the water, a behavior called 'breaching'.

or baleen whales. Instead of teeth, their mouths contain hundreds of hard plates of baleen. Together, these act as a huge strainer with which the whale sifts small prey from the surrounding water. Currently, there are 13 recognized species of baleen whales, although it is very likely that this number will grow as genetic studies sort out which species should be split further.

Right whales are baleen whales. They are part of a group called the *balaenids* which include four species: three right whales and the bowhead whale. The bowhead is found only in the Northern Hemisphere and spends most of its life associated with sea ice in the Arctic.

Until recently, scientists recognized two (not three) species of right whale, termed 'northern' and 'southern'. Indeed, some scientists went further and suggested that all right whales should be grouped together as a single species. The northern right whales were those in the North Atlantic and North Pacific, while the southern right whales inhabited the Southern Hemisphere. Recently, however, genetic analysis conducted by Howard Rosenbaum and colleagues has indicated that the right whales in these three major ocean regions are separate species, and they have been duly classified as such.

The definition of what makes a 'species' is still debated in science. The old definition dictated that if two animals of the opposite sex could mate and produce viable offspring, then they should be considered as belonging to the same species. But this ignores the fact that some populations are separated by great distances or insurmountable geographical barriers, and thus are never able to mix and breed. If two populations have been thus separated for thousands of years or longer, they often develop distinct genetic differences; more significantly, their lack of mixing for so long may mean that they are now on two (or more) very different evolutionary paths.

This seems to be the case with right whales. Even though right whales everywhere look very similar to one another, genetic analysis tells us that they have been separated for a very long time. Accordingly, today we talk about the North Atlantic right whale, the North Pacific right whale, and the southern right whale. Each is regarded as a distinct species, and each has its own scientific name.

A right whale breaks the surface to breathe, with one of its huge flippers visible underwater.

'True Whale of the Ice'

Anyone seeing a right whale for the first time could be forgiven for entertaining uncharitable thoughts about the animal's appearance. By any measure, they are odd-looking beasts: robust in form (some would say 'fat'), with a very broad black back, no dorsal fin and a huge head that is covered with strange horny growths called callosities. The tail, however, is magnificent: a great black triangle that is usually raised high in the air whenever the animal dives deeply.

Right whales are huge animals. While not as long or as sleek as the great blue and fin whales, they can reach lengths of 60 feet (more than 18 meters). Since right whales are so stocky, they also weigh more per unit of length than other whales: the largest right whales on record were more than 100 tons. As in most of the baleen whales, female right whales are larger than males: although the difference is not large (about 5 feet, or 1.5 meters, in adults), the difference between the sexes is quite consistent. It is not clear why females should be the larger of the two sexes, though this probably relates to differing energetic needs. Because reproduction is such an energetic drain on females, it is likely that they have evolved a somewhat larger size to permit greater energy storage during the time that they must nurse a calf.

Another minor mystery about right whales is that those in the North Pacific are larger than their Southern Hemisphere counterparts. In other baleen whales (for example, blue and fin whales), the southern populations contain, on average, somewhat larger animals than those found in the Northern Hemisphere. We have no idea why North Pacific right whales are the exception to this rule.

Right whales are all black above, while the coloration on their underside varies

Beside a human diver, the huge size of a right whale's head becomes evident.

from mostly black in some animals to mostly white in others. Beneath this layer of skin – which in places can be almost an inch (2.4 cm) thick – is one of the most substantial layers of blubber of any whale. For all whales, blubber serves two purposes: as heat conservation and energy storage. The thick layer of fat in which the animal's body is encased allows it to live in very cold waters; since water absorbs heat many times faster than air, aquatic mammals must have much better insulation than their terrestrial counterparts. Blubber also allows the whale to survive prolonged periods without food. In the largest right whales, the blubber is up to a foot (30 cm) thick; the only animal with more is the bowhead, whose arctic lifestyle requires a fat layer that can be almost two feet (60 cm) thick.

The huge head of a right whale makes up almost a third of the animal's size. It is characterized by large, deeply arched jaws and a vast mouth. As in all whales, the nostrils ('blowholes') are located on top of the head, and are preceded by a ridge of tissue that serves as a splashguard. Like all baleen whales, right whales have two nostrils (in toothed whales, by contrast, there is only one). The blow of a right whale is very distinctive when seen from directly ahead or behind the whale: because the two nostrils are quite widely separated, the blow has an unmistakable V shape.

One of the most distinctive features of a right whale's head is the presence of the callosities. These are patches of what is known as 'cornified epithelium' (hardened skin) that are raised and often sharply ridged. It is interesting to note that the callosities are found in the same places that one finds hair in a human being: on top of the head, on the upper and lower lips, on the chin, behind the nostrils and above the eyes. The callosities are naturally black or gray in color, but they usually appear yellow or red; this is because they are colonized by millions of parasites called cyamids, or 'whale lice', which give the callosities their color. These tiny crustaceans eat dead skin, and they may also use the whale as a base from which to feed on

The yellowish growths on the head are called callosities,
and can be used to identify individual whales.

*The partly open mouth of a feeding right whale shows the
rack of baleen hanging down from its upper jaw.*

microscopic organisms in the surrounding water. As we will see, the pattern of callosities on each right whale is unique to that animal, like a fingerprint, and this very useful characteristic has allowed scientists to easily identify and track individual whales.

Inside the whale's mouth, two great racks of baleen plates hang from the upper jaw, one on each side. In each rack there are between 220 and 260 plates, almost all of which are black in color. At up to 10 feet (3 meters), right whale baleen is exceeded in length only by that of the bowhead whale. The long plates are narrow and tapered, and the inside margin of each one is fringed by fine, silky hair. As we will see in a later chapter, this hair is the key to the remarkable filtration system that allows right whales to eat some of the smallest food in the ocean.

Also inside the mouth is the whale's huge tongue, which can weigh more than a ton. The tongue is not very muscular, and is far less mobile than ours, being attached to the bottom of the whale's mouth.

The right whale's two flippers are large, broad and paddle-shaped. As in all whales, an X-ray of the flipper would reveal an internal bone structure resembling that of a huge hand, with four 'fingers' that testify to the original terrestrial ancestry of cetaceans. As we move back along the whale, we find the body tapering towards the great tail, which (unlike in fish) is set in a horizontal plane and moves up and down to power the animal's swimming. In the largest right whales, this tail is almost 20 feet (6 meters) wide from tip to tip.

Right whales are found in the North Atlantic, the North Pacific and over much of the Southern Hemisphere. As we have noted, each of these geographically separate groups is today considered its own species. All three belong in the genus *Eubalaena*, which means 'true whale'. The North Pacific right whale is *Eubalaena japonica* ('of Japan'), and the southern right whale is *Eubalaena australis* ('southern').

The scientific name for the North Atlantic right whale is the original name that was once given to all three species, *Eubalaena glacialis*. This name means 'true whale of the ice', and in that name lies a sad irony. Before whaling, North Atlantic right whales were found commonly in high latitudes in icy waters such as those off Greenland. However, they were virtually extirpated from these portions of their historic range, and the scientific name is accurate no longer.

Many people consider that right whales are characterized by a distribution that is largely coastal. It is true that big aggregations of right whales are often found in shallower waters near the coast or on the continental shelf, and in some places they frequently come within miles or even yards of the shore. However, our view of them as a coastal species is not really accurate, and reflects the fact that it is much easier for scientists to look for these whales in coastal waters than in dangerous habitats far out to sea. Southern right whales spend long periods hundreds of miles from land, and we know from the logbooks of 19th-century whaling ships that right whales were often found in the deep-water realms of both the North Atlantic and North Pacific Oceans.

Sadly, today much of this range has been lost through the immense damage inflicted by whaling. In the North Atlantic, right whales once ranged from Europe to Iceland and Greenland, down the Canadian coast to New England, and as far south as northwestern Africa. Today, the small population that remains feeds largely in an area that encompasses the Gulf of Maine, the Bay of Fundy and the shelf waters off Nova Scotia; the only known calving ground for this population is off Florida and Georgia in the southeastern United States. Right whales occasionally appear elsewhere in the North Atlantic, but such sightings are comparatively rare today.

Similarly, the original range of the right whale covered most of the North Pacific basin, from the Gulf of Alaska to the Okhotsk Sea, including deep-water areas far from land. Today, this range has shrunk to a small fraction of what it once was.

In the Southern Hemisphere, where right whale populations are today in much better condition, right whales are found over a greater portion of their historic range, from Antarctica to the coastal waters of Australia, southern Africa and South America. However, whaling removed them from many places, and in some historically important areas they have only recently begun to stage a comeback.

One such place is the remote Auckland Islands, south of New Zealand. As is the case for many historical right whale habitats, the animals there aggregated in large numbers and were densely packed together in small bays. This created an ideal situation for whalers, who quickly wiped out the animals gathered there. For

A right whale lying on its side shows one of its huge paddle-shaped flippers.

decades, right whales were largely absent from the Auckland Islands; but as the population elsewhere began to expand, whales finally rediscovered this old habitat and began to appear there once more. Recently, surveys conducted by Nathalie Patenaude and her colleagues have found large numbers of right whales in the region.

It is a sign of the population's recovery, and a phenomenon which we hope will be repeated in other habitats from which right whales were extirpated by whaling.

Individuals

In the 1970s, a revolution occurred in the field of whale biology. As scientists began to work with living whales rather than with carcasses supplied by the whaling industry, they suddenly realized that, in many species, patterns of natural markings could be used to recognize individuals. We take this technique for granted in our own species, where facial and other features allow us to recognize friends and acquaintances; and of course fingerprints have long provided law enforcement officials with a reliable tool to identify individuals. But studies of wild animals based upon individual recognition were few and far between until fairly recently.

When you can tell individual animals apart, you can suddenly conduct all kinds of studies that are not possible otherwise. You can track the reproductive rates of individual females, study who associates with whom, examine individual patterns of residency and return in an area, and – by photographing individuals in two or more places – can track long-range movements. In contrast, if you don't know whether the whales you see today are the same or different from those you saw yesterday, you are very limited in what you can learn about their habits.

Right whales were actually the first large whale for which this method was developed. In 1968 Bob Brownell discovered a population of southern right whales in the waters off Peninsula Valdes, Argentina. The following year Roger Payne began a study of these animals, and quickly discovered that he could tell them apart by the pattern of callosities on their heads. By photographing these patterns, as well as any scars or other unusual marks elsewhere on an animal's body, he could assemble a unique 'fingerprint' for that individual that would allow him to recognize it in subsequent encounters.

Payne's southern right whale project continues today, the longest continuously running study of individual whales anywhere in the world. Over the next ten years, many other individual-based studies were begun on other species, and as a result we now know a great deal about the biology and behavior of many whale populations.

In the North Atlantic, all observations of individually identified right whales are sent to the New England Aquarium, which curates the North Atlantic Right Whale Catalog. This catalog contains thousands of photographs and associated sighting data gathered over more than two decades by numerous researchers. If you look through the sighting histories of individuals in this catalog, the first thing that is immediately obvious is that different whales are not alike in their patterns of occurrence and movement. Some individuals are seen very frequently year after year, while others make only rare appearances.

For example, catalog number 1014 -- a female -- was first observed in 1974, and was seen every year from 1979 on; but she has been observed primarily in Massachusetts Bay in winter or spring, and only very occasionally in the population's major known summer feeding ground in the Bay of Fundy. In contrast, an adult male numbered 1032 has been seen in the Bay of Fundy every summer since he was first sighted in 1980.

The sighting history of catalog number 1412, another adult female, stands in sharp contrast to both of these animals. She has been seen only twice, in 1984 and 1997, on both occasions in an area called Jeffrey's Ledge off Cape Ann, Massachusetts, and on both occasions with a calf next to her. Her whereabouts during the 13 years between these sightings – and the years since – is a mystery.

There are a number of right whales in the catalog who disappear like this for long periods. Occasionally they are photographed in far-flung places well outside the 'normal' range of this population: for example, catalog number 1718 has been seen only twice, once off Iceland in 1987 and then again in a well-known habitat off the coast of Nova Scotia two years later. Where do whales like 1412 and 1718 live for the rest of the time between these fleeting observations? We do not know. They might be the remnants of a vanishing group of whales whose ancestors were once abundant in remoter habitats in the North Atlantic before whaling wiped them out.

One of the dubious benefits of dealing with a small population like that of the North Atlantic right whale is that the scientists working with these animals can recognize most of the individuals in the population on sight. Marilyn Marx, Amy Knowlton, Lisa Conger and Philip Hamilton of the New England Aquarium have much or all of the right whale catalog in their heads, and instantly recognize most of the animals that they encounter in the field. These biologists are as

An albino right whale calf. Albinos are quite rare.

familiar with the different behaviors and life histories of their study subjects as they are with those of their friends, and they are more aware than anyone that right whales, like all animals, have different 'personalities'. Some are curious and playful, while others are more businesslike and show no interest in boats or humans. Some have distinctive feeding styles. And some females are reliable mothers, returning every three or four years with a new calf in tow.

They know the rarely seen whales, too; and finding one is a moment of great excitement. A whale with the catalog number 1035 had not been seen since 1986,

This right whale's (right) eye is wide open. The whale's vision is good, but is limited by the murky water in which it lives.

and was presumed to have died. Then in 2002 Marilyn Marx was looking over photographs of right whales taken that spring by a National Marine Fisheries Service aerial survey. To her amazement, there was 1035, who had mysteriously reappeared after an absence of 16 years. Then the following spring, Marilyn was on a research vessel east of Cape Cod, and approached a right whale to identify it. As it surfaced, she screamed excitedly – it was 1035 again. Neither she nor anyone else knows where this animal had been during the 16 years that it (we still don't know its sex) was 'missing'.

But perhaps the most remarkable story is that of another infrequently seen animal, a female with the catalog number 1045. This animal had been seen in only four years, with long gaps in between: first in 1959, then again in 1980, 1985 and finally in 1992 (when I photographed her on a cold March day in Cape Cod Bay). Then one day someone sent to the New England Aquarium a photocopy of an old newspaper article from Florida. The article was about a mother and calf right whale that had been pursued by hunters; the calf was killed, but the mother escaped. The article included a photo of the mother, and since the animal was distinctively marked the Aquarium staff decided – mostly for the fun of it – to run the image through the right whale catalog.

To their amazement, they found a match: it was 1045. What made this record remarkable was the date of the newspaper article: 1935. It is likely that 1045's calf was the last right whale to be killed in the North Atlantic before the species was protected that year.

How old was 1045? Following the newspaper match, she was observed once more, in 1995. Assuming that she had been at least ten years old in 1935 (old enough to have a calf), she would have been at least 70 when last seen. We know now from this remarkable chance match that right whales are long-lived animals; and in 1045's case, she was an old whale with a very bad memory of human beings. Sadly, when last seen in 1995 she had a serious head injury, evidently the result of a collision with a ship. She has not been seen since, and is assumed to be dead.

Of course, photo-identification is not the only technique that we use to study right whales. More sophisticated technology has recently been applied to our investigations of these animals. In particular, genetic analysis tells us a great deal about populations of right whales in both the Northern and Southern Hemispheres. Samples for this work are usually obtained in the form of skin biopsies, generally by shooting a small dart at the whale. The dart harmlessly takes a small punch of skin before bouncing off into the water, in which it floats for easy retrieval. Back in the laboratory, DNA extracted from the skin tissue can be used to answer questions which often cannot be addressed in any other way. Genetic studies can tell us about population structure, evolutionary history, paternity of offspring, social relationships and many other aspects of a whale's biology and behavior. The sexes of sampled individuals are routinely determined using a genetic technique. And, as noted earlier, genetic analysis lay behind the recent decision to recognize three species of right whales.

Nor is genetic analysis limited to samples from the present time. DNA can be extracted from museum specimens of bone or baleen, including centuries-old samples. Brad White, Moira Brown and Howard Rosenbaum have all used this technique successfully on old right whale samples, including bones salvaged from the 16th-century Basque whaling site at Red Bay, Labrador. Using these historical samples, these scientists can examine the extent to which extensive whaling caused a loss of genetic diversity in the population. Indeed, after centuries of exploitation, we find that North Atlantic right whales are today very inbred relative to larger, healthier whale populations; whether this has negative consequences for their recovery is not yet clear.

*The vast tail of this right whale breaks the surface together with
the tip of the whale's head. The tail can be up to 20ft (6 meters) wide.*

Feeding: And the Largest Shall Prey Upon the Smallest

Right whales are among the largest animals on earth; indeed, they are among the largest animals that have ever lived. They are longer than most dinosaurs and, at a maximum weight of 100 tons, they are heavier than even the largest of those great prehistoric reptiles.

One might expect huge animals to have a diet consisting of large prey, and yet this is not the case with any of the baleen whales. Even the largest whale – the mighty blue – feeds on small prey, subsisting as it does mainly on shrimp-sized krill. In right whales, we are presented with an even more extreme contrast: for here is one of the largest animals in the world making its living by consuming one of the smallest of all creatures: the humble copepod.

Copepods are part of a huge and staggeringly abundant group of marine animals that are collectively known as zooplankton. The word *plankton* comes from a Greek word meaning 'to roam or drift'. Plankton are indeed the great drifters: they include any life in the ocean whose movements are at the whim of the tides and currents. Marine biologists divide plankton into two groups: *phytoplankton* and *zooplankton*. Phytoplankton are microscopic plants, and like plants on land they convert sunlight into energy. They are the foundation of every food chain in the ocean; without them, life in the marine realm would cease to exist. Zooplankton are tiny animals, and like phytoplankton they come in a breathtaking multiplicity of forms.

Zooplankton are the tiny grazers of the ocean, collectively consuming vast quantities of phytoplankton (and, for some predatory species, smaller zooplankton). In turn, zooplankton provide food for innumerable animals higher up in the food chain, including fish and – in some cases – whales.

The popular idea that all whales feed on plankton is actually not correct. Many species, such as the humpback and fin whale, eat small fish and krill. Gray whales eat many things, including mud-dwelling invertebrates such as amphipods. And sperm whales – the only great whales that have teeth – prey largely on squids which range in size from quite small to truly enormous.

Right whales, however, are true plankton feeders. They subsist on various species, but the largest component of their diet consists of animals known as copepods, notably those belonging to the genus *Calanus*. These tiny animals are about the size of a grain of rice, and marine biologists estimate that they are the most abundant animal in the ocean.

Copepods are typically found in patches which in some cases contain billions of organisms. These patches vary considerably in size and density: some are small and sparse, others extensive and thick. Research by Charles Mayo and his colleagues at the Center for Coastal Studies in Massachusetts has shown that right whales do not feed randomly on any copepod patch that comes their way. On the contrary, they seek out particularly dense patches, where the concentration of these tiny animals sometimes exceeds a staggering 20,000,000 organisms per cubic meter! Mayo's research has suggested that there is a minimum acceptable copepod density, below which a right whale simply does not consider it worthwhile to open its mouth: this density is somewhere around 1000-3000 organisms per cubic meter.

Like many baleen whales, right whales may not feed year-round. There is good evidence that at least some animals – in particular those females that migrate to warmer waters to calve – fast during the winter, living off the huge reserves of fat stored in their blubber. But for most of the year, right whales are in the colder waters of temperate or high latitudes, and there they spend much of their time eating.

How right whales locate copepod patches, and how they assess whether the density of a patch is acceptable, is not known. It is an interesting question. Unlike toothed whales such as dolphins, right whales and other baleen whales do not possess a biological sonar with which to remotely detect prey. Consequently, how right whales find their food is largely a mystery, although we can perhaps hazard an educated guess.

Copepods are not distributed randomly throughout the ocean; on the contrary, they are much more likely to be concentrated in certain areas than others. Since copepods consume (among other things) phytoplankton, and since phytoplankton need sunlight and nutrients to grow and reproduce, both are much more likely to occur close to the surface, and in locations where nutrients abound. Many places fit these requirements, but areas known as upwelling zones are particularly rich in

Two right whales seen head on, their callosities clearly visible. Despite their bulk, they move very gracefully through the water.

life. Here, nutrients which have fallen to the seafloor are returned to the surface, often in areas where the topography of the bottom or some other physical feature forces currents to sweep upwards. At the surface, the nutrients become available to phytoplankton, which in turn attract zooplankton such as copepods. It is very likely that right whales can detect the particular set of oceanographic or habitat characteristics – such as topography or current patterns – that mark a potentially productive feeding area.

A right whale engages in 'sailing' behavior, placing its
huge tail in the air and drifting downwind.

As right whales grow older, their accumulated store of experience allows them to return to places which served them well in the past; in other words, they remember where the good feeding grounds are. These places will vary in their productivity from year to year as oceanographic conditions change: sometimes they will be rich in prey, while on other occasions they will prove largely barren. Like many animals, right whales engage in a behavior called 'prospecting', where they periodically travel around potential feeding areas to assess the quantity and quality of the prey in each. If conditions are good, they remain and feed; if not, they move on to the next habitat.

So for a right whale, finding food is all a matter of scale. At the largest scale, the whale must find its way back to a particular feeding ground. Then it must locate a potentially productive area within that ground, then somehow detect and assess actual patches of zooplankton. How right whales find these patches, which are often widely distributed in space, is not known. Perhaps they narrow their search by traveling along temperature gradients, or perhaps they have chemoreceptors that allow them to detect prey at a distance in the water column.

One other possibility is that right whales have retained a workable sense of smell in air. The olfactory lobe of a baleen whale's brain is quite large; in contrast, the lobe is now only a rudimentary structure in the brain of toothed whales. This is not surprising, because a toothed whale with an efficient sonar system would no longer require a sense of smell, especially since odors are largely undetectable underwater. But for right whales and other mysticetes, smell may play an important role in finding food, when that food is present in concentrations at the surface. If you are on a boat and find yourself downwind of a large patch of plankton, you will certainly smell it – plankton has a quite distinct and not unpleasant odor. It would be surprising if baleen whales had not retained the ability to use this simple but effective cue in finding their food.

Once a whale is swimming within a plankton patch, it must go about the actual business of consuming its food. Right whales are skim feeders: they open their mouths and move through their food, continuously filtering it from seawater as they go. This is different from some other whales (for example, humpbacks and blue whales) which are 'gulpers': these animals feed in discrete events, engulfing large quantities of water and food, straining the food and then moving on to take another 'gulp.'

Water enters a right whale's mouth at the front and passes through the two great racks of baleen that hang down the upper jaw, one to each side. There are from 220 to 260 baleen plates in each rack, stacked side by side. The inside of each plate is fringed with fine, silky hair, and together the hair from these hundreds of plates makes up a screen which acts as a remarkably efficient filter. Tiny copepods enter the whale's mouth with the water, then are trapped against the mat of hair on the inside of the baleen, while the water passes through the filter and leaves the whale's mouth through the small spaces between the baleen plates. Somehow whales periodically 'clean' the inside of the baleen and swallow their prey, but the details of exactly how this is accomplished are not clear.

How much a right whale eats during the course of a typical day is not well understood. It is generally assumed that large whales consume about 3-4% of their body weight each day. If this is true, then an average adult right whale weighing about 40 tons would eat somewhere from one to one and a half *tons* of copepods a day. That these marine giants can make a living from such tiny fare is testament not only to the efficiency of a right whale's foraging and filtering abilities, but also to the extraordinary abundance of life in the world's oceans.

A right whale skim-feeds through a plankton patch. The huge mouth can process vast quantities of water as the whale filters copepods and other prey through its baleen.

Reproduction, Behavior and Social Structure

Like most baleen whales, female right whales have a pregnancy that lasts about a year. There is a distinct season for giving birth, which is winter: calves are typically born between December and March. In the North Atlantic, the only known calving ground lies in the warm coastal waters of Florida and Georgia in the southeastern United States, although it is likely that a second ground once existed at Cintra Bay on the western coast of North Africa. Similarly, in the Southern Hemisphere, calves enter the world in relatively warm water in habitats off the coasts of South Africa, Australia and South America. We have very little idea where North Pacific right whales go to give birth: sightings in mid-winter are rare, although there is a suggestion from historical whaling data that the calving grounds for this species may lie far from land.

Not surprisingly, a right whale is not a small creature when it begins its life. Big animals have big babies, and right whale babies are among the largest on earth. An average right whale calf is about 14 feet (4.3 meters) in length at birth, and weighs about half a ton. No one has ever witnessed a right whale birth, but it is likely that the event is quite quick. Calves are precocious and begin to swim immediately, and shortly after birth they will begin to feed on their mother's milk.

Female right whales have two mammary glands located on either side of the genital opening, on the underside of the body back towards the tail. Nursing in all whales is not simply a question of passive suckling by the calf; rather it is an active process on the part of the mother. Each mammary gland contains a compressor muscle, which allows the mother to actually pump milk into the calf's mouth; presumably this minimizes the amount of seawater that is incidentally ingested by her offspring. Whale milk is extremely rich, containing more than six times the fat of human or cow milk, and right whale calves consume perhaps 50 gallons (190 liters) a day.

After a few days or weeks in the calving area, mothers take their calves on a long migration to the feeding grounds of higher latitudes. There, a female will eat as much as possible to make up for the great energetic cost of lactation, while her calf continues to nurse for some months more. Calves are weaned at anywhere from six to eighteen months of age; the average is about a year. Shortly after weaning, mother and calf separate, although whether this event is initiated by the female or her offspring is not known.

Once she is alone again, a mature female will usually not calve again for a while. The average interval between births in right whales is three years, which is rather longer than for some other baleen whales.

Although the mother/calf bond is very tight during the calf's natal year, a female will reassociate only infrequently with her offspring in later years. This is typical of baleen whales, which are not as strongly social as many other animals. Although their association patterns are far from random, they do not show the tight social structure that we see in many toothed whales. In some killer whales, for example, animals remain together in family groups for their entire lives; the same is true for pilot whales. In these and many other odontocete species, bonds are tight and kinship is everything.

If you were to follow a right whale around for a day, you would probably see it associate with several different individuals for short periods of time. Occasionally, you might see two or three right whales feeding together, moving with mouths open through a patch of prey in what is called an 'echelon' formation. And in many places, you would have a good chance of watching your chosen whale engaging in sexual activity at some point during the day.

One of the mysteries about right whales is that they appear to have sex year-round. While this may not seem strange to humans, it is unusual in baleen whales. With a one-year gestation and a calving season that is confined to the winter, in theory whales should be mating only during this winter period. This is largely true for some other species. For example, mating in humpback whales is a strongly seasonal activity: whales mate in winter, and one year later females give birth to the calves that have resulted from those brief unions.

Right whales, however, are different: they mate throughout the year, in virtually every one of the habitats in which they are found.

Nor is mating confined to the modest union of one male and one female. Female right whales will often mate serially with multiple partners, and have even been observed to copulate with two males at the same time. What is behind this strangely promiscuous behavior?

The vast number of organisms that reproduce

Males compete to mate with a female.

sexually (rather than asexually) do so through a bewildering array of mating systems, but in all species the manner in which animals go about seeking and securing mates is governed by a single underlying principle: maximizing individual reproductive success. Put simply, each individual animal – whether furred, feathered or anything else – ultimately wants to leave as many copies of its genes in future generations as it can. But since the environments in which these species live vary greatly, so do mating systems. As a general rule, environment governs how mature females will be distributed, and this in turn largely determines the distribution of breeding males. If females concentrate because food or shelter during the mating season is confined to small areas, then males will aggregate in those locations too. In contrast, if resources are widely scattered, then females will be also — and so will males. Different situations produce very different mating strategies for both sexes.

Mating systems vary from monogamy (partners mate only with each other) and polygny (males mate with more than one female) to polyandry (females mate with more than one male) and promiscuity (where both sexes mate with multiple partners).

Females may solicit males, sometimes by flippering.

A species' mating system can often be predicted from knowledge of a number of factors, and one of these is the size of the testes in males, relative to body size. Primates provide a good example. Gorillas are large animals, but have very small testes; this is because the dominant male in a gorilla group is the only male who has sexual access to the females in that group, and as a result he needs to produce just enough sperm to fertilize his mates. Chimpanzees, however, are very different: here, females mate with multiple partners, sometimes in quick succession. Consequently, chimpanzees have huge testes for their size; chimpanzee males must produce large quantities of sperm to outcompete that of any other males that recently copulated with the same female. This system is known as sperm competition, and it is known to occur in innumerable species, from insects to birds to mammals.

If we look at how big a whale's testes are relative to its body size, we find surprising differences among species. Blue whales – the largest of all animals – have very small testes for their size: they typically weigh about 44 lb (20 kg). While this may seem large, in relative terms it is not – and it pales in comparison to the equivalent figure for the right whale.

Right whales possess the largest testes in the animal kingdom. Even though male right whales may be half the size of a male blue whale, they have a pair of testes that tip the scales at the astonishing weight of one ton!

Given this, it is not difficult to predict that the mating system of right whales must involve sperm competition. And indeed this is the case. As noted above, females will mate serially with two or more males. Unlike in some other species (for example, humpback whales) in which males aggressively fight over mates, male right whales compete rather less at the individual level but instead through production of huge volumes of sperm.

Right whale courtship groups often involve one female and two or more males; on occasion, these groups contain more than 30 animals, with the males all jostling for position next to the female. There is evidence that females use vocalizations to 'call in' males to these groups, thus presumably inciting competition. A large courtship group is a seething mass of bodies, with males twisting and turning as they attempt to get close to the female in the middle. Quite what females think about all this is not known, but a courted female will often roll upside down between breaths. Some scientists have interpreted this as an attempt to avoid copulation, and it may indeed be so in cases where the female does not consider the male concerned to be a suitable partner. However, in other cases a female will lie upside-down quite passively while a male mates with her.

The act of mating itself is quite passive in nature. Like some other mammals (notably ungulates), the penis of a male right whale is fibro-elastic rather than vascular, and the organ is both flexible and mobile. A male and female lie side by side and the male's penis reaches over her body, with the tip inserted into her vagina. Because of this flexibility, it is physically possible for two males to mate at the same time, with one on each side of the female.

So why do right whales mate in summer, a time when they are presumably not conceiving? In some mammals, females will mate at one time and store sperm until environmental conditions are better able to support a pregnancy. In others, there is a delay in the implantation of the egg in the uterus for similar reasons. However, there is no evidence that either of these strategies occur in any cetacean. The only plausible explanation for a right whale's prolific sex life is that mating serves a social function. Perhaps females use these events to assess the condition and quality of males, and remember these assessments later in the year when it is time for them to conceive.

When not eating or mating, right whales engage in a variety of other behaviors. The most spectacular of these is breaching, in which a whale will jump out of the water, returning to the surface with a tremendous splash. Breaching may serve several purposes depending on the context: it may be a way of signaling position to other whales, or it may be excitement or play.

Finally, one of the most interesting behaviors observed in right whales is 'sailing'. To date, this has been seen only in southern right whales, and was first documented off the coast of Argentina by Roger Payne. There, right whales raise their huge tails into the air like a great sail and slowly drift with the wind. Often, a sailing right whale will drift for some distance downwind and then swim back to its starting point to begin all over again. Whether this behavior serves any function is not clear; it may simply be a rather whimsical form of entertainment for this giant of the seas.

The Right Whale to Kill

Right whales have the dubious distinction of having the longest hunting history of any species of large whale. We do not know when or where the first right whale was intentionally killed by human hunters brave enough to attempt the task. In the year 890, an adventurer by the name of Ottar returned to Saxon England from a voyage of discovery to the White Sea and reported to King Alfred that Norwegians in the town of Trømso killed huge whales. It is possible that these were right whales, but whether this hunt was a regular occurrence for profit, or simply an opportunistic hunt to meet local needs, is not clear. The first records of what was clearly commercial (for-profit) whaling come from southern France and northern Spain, where the Basque people began to hunt right whales around the 11th century. Medieval records give us some interesting insights into this period, recording market trade in whale products and tax levies. One such record tells us that the king of France imposed a tax on the tongues of right whales sold in the city of Bayonne in southern France; evidently the tongue was considered a delicacy, and sold well in local markets (though having seen more whale tongues than I care to count, I can't imagine why!)

The hunt was clearly well organized. Watch towers were set up to look for whales along the coastline. When whales were sighted, they were pursued in open boats and struck with metal harpoons. This must have been a protracted and dangerous exercise, with boats being towed behind – and occasionally overturned or smashed by – wounded whales. Nonetheless, the fishermen of this region became so proficient at the business of whaling that for centuries Basque harpooners were sought by all European whaling nations. Indeed, so valuable were the Basques to this fishery that a king of Spain once issued an edict forbidding them, on pain of death, to take employment in the service of any other country.

Of the various species of whales which frequented the coastal waters of south-western Europe, the right whale was by far the best choice as a target for whaling. They often approached close to the coast where they could be easily seen and pursued. In addition, right whales are slow animals; unlike the fast and sleek fin or blue whales, they could be overtaken by men in boats powered by oars or sails. Two other characteristics made them preferred prey: they usually floated when killed, and they yielded a huge quantity of valuable oil. Because right whales have such thick blubber, they are positively buoyant, and any right whale in good condition will not sink when it dies. This is not the case for some other species. If whalers managed to catch and kill a fin whale – never an easy task to begin with – the carcass would sink, forcing the whalers to wait for several days until the gases of decomposition might bring the whale back to the surface. Even then, the chances that the body would be found were poor.

Not so with right whales. Whalers could kill several animals and then tow them back to land for butchering. Afterwards, the meat would have been sold in markets for human consumption, and the oil rendered from boiling the whale's thick blubber served to light thousands of lamps in medieval Europe.

It is because of all these favorable (to the whalers) characteristics that the right whale obtained its common name: it was, quite simply, the right whale to kill.

The right whale's great vulnerability inevitably led to its demise at a time when no consideration was given to the idea of a sustainable hunt for anything. This decline was almost certainly accelerated by the Basques' preference for taking mothers and their calves. A calf was easy to kill and, in so doing, the whalers would be likely to also capture the mother because of the latter's tendency to remain with her offspring. But this habit of killing both calves and reproductively mature females was fatal to the population's future.

By the beginning of the 16th century, the Basques had begun to seek other whaling grounds, and they were almost certainly among the first explorers of the mysterious New World discovered on the other side of the Atlantic Ocean. When this expansion began is not known, but by 1530 Basque whalers were observed at anchor at Red Bay in southern Labrador. There, we know from archaeological evidence that they pursued both right and bowhead whales; the range of the latter species seems to have extended further south than it does today during a period of cold climate known as the Little Ice Age.

By this time or shortly afterwards, the relentless hunting of North Atlantic right whales across much of their range was taking a toll on the population. By the early 1700s, European records suggest that a substantial decline had occurred in the abundance of right whales, and it is likely that this began much

A right whale puts its head above the water – 'spy-hopping'.

earlier. Also at this time, right whaling had become an established activity off the east coast of what is now the United States. Whaling on a small scale probably began in New England sometime after the Pilgrims landed in 1620, became far more regular and well-organized by 1700, and subsequently expanded to other coastal areas of the colonies.

In the 19th century, the whaling industry in New England reached the peak of its activity and wealth. Vessels from New England ports such as Nantucket and New Bedford sailed far afield to other oceans on three- or four-year voyages in pursuit of whales. During this period, huge numbers of southern right whales were killed, and virtually all populations of this austral species were decimated.

Other whalers, however, plied a more 'local' trade within the wide confines of the North Atlantic, searching for humpback, sperm and right whales on shorter trips lasting a few months or a year. It was these latter whalers who did considerable damage to the remaining populations of the North Atlantic right whale, killing animals as far north as Greenland and as far south as northwestern Africa.

Right whales were prized for oil and baleen.

For the European population, which had fought a long battle for survival during centuries of exploitation in the eastern Atlantic, the combination of continued catches in high latitudes and a spate of kills at the probable calving ground at Cintra Bay was devastating. The final phase of this population's demise began in 1881, when Norwegian whalers discovered previously unknown aggregations of right whales off Scotland and Iceland. Over the next four decades, these last survivors of a once-large population were wiped out, and with their passing right whales effectively became extinct in the eastern North Atlantic.

In 1935, the hunting of right whales was banned (at least in theory) worldwide, and while this protection came too late for the eastern population, it may have saved the species in the western North Atlantic. Today, a small population survives there, but as we shall see in the next chapter its ultimate survival still hangs in the balance.

Meanwhile, the North Pacific right whale enjoyed comparative safety from whaling until 1835. In that year, an American whaler named the *Ganges* arrived in the Gulf of Alaska and the captain reported seeing 'a million whales'. While this was clearly an exaggeration, it was testament to the size of the largely unexploited stock of right whales in the North Pacific. However, once word of the bounty became known, whalers wasted no time. Just 14 years later, right whales had become sufficiently uncommon in the eastern North Pacific that many whalers turned their attention instead to recently discovered populations of bowhead whales in the Arctic. Then a westward expansion of the whaling fleet discovered new stocks of both right whales and bowheads in the western Pacific, notably in the Okhotsk Sea, and these were quickly depleted. By 1900 the North Pacific right whale population had been reduced to a fraction of its former size, and there were only sporadic catches of this species up until the 1935 ban on all right whaling.

Had this situation persisted, it is likely that North Pacific right whales would today be enjoying a slow recovery. That they are not (at least in the eastern North Pacific) is due to one of the most shameful episodes in the history of modern wildlife management.

In 1946, the whaling nations together signed the International Convention for the Regulation of Whaling, a treaty which also created the International Whaling Commission (IWC). The IWC was established to oversee research on whales, and to use that research to conduct assessments of the various populations with a view to better managing their exploitation. The IWC's effectiveness was severely diminished by the whaling nations' consistent refusal to accept evidence of declining populations until it was too late. Protection was eventually given to many species, but often only after numbers had been drastically reduced. As it turned out, the situation was even worse than anyone imagined.

Beginning in 1948, the Soviet Union began a massive and highly secret campaign of illegal whaling across much of the world's oceans, killing whales regardless of their age, size or protected status. When this gross breach of international agreements was finally revealed after the Cold War ended, it was discovered that almost 100,000 whales had been illegally caught in the Southern Hemisphere alone. The total included more than 3000 'protected' southern right whales. And the damage done to at least one population north of the equator was potentially even greater.

In 1995, I was working with Bob Brownell on a review of all 20th-century sightings, strandings and catches of North Pacific right whales. During the review, we noticed that the numbers of right whales seen each year in the eastern North Pacific remained relatively constant until 1963, when suddenly sightings of the species plummeted. In almost any year prior to 1964, there were more sightings in this area than in the period 1964 to 2004 combined. Clearly some catastrophe lay behind this dramatic decline; and sadly, it wasn't hard to guess what this catastrophe was.

Enquiries with former Soviet whale biologists were made, and finally revealed that the USSR had killed 372 right whales in the eastern North Pacific, primarily over a three-year period. Catches were made in the Gulf of Alaska, the Aleutian Islands and the Bering Sea. Incredibly, the total number of these catches probably represented the bulk of the remnant population, and they dealt a devastating blow from which it may not recover.

The Soviet illegal catches were simply the most recent of a long series of insults suffered by right whales worldwide. Indeed, the relentless exploitation to which right whales were subject for so many centuries is the reason for their often critically endangered status today. Sadly, as we shall see in the next chapter, while the hunting of right whales has finally ceased, other problems have now taken the place of whaling as a threat to their recovery.

Right whales were hunted throughout the world, beginning almost a thousand years ago.
Their slow speed and proximity to shore made them easy targets for early whalers.

Conservation and the Future

By the time that the International Whaling Commission finally enacted a moratorium on all commercial whaling in 1986, the irresponsibility of many whaling nations had reduced the majority of whale populations to small fractions of their original sizes, and left several on the brink of extinction. The mighty blue whale, which once numbered a quarter million animals in the vast open waters of the Southern Ocean, is today reduced to perhaps a thousand individuals there, and a few thousand more elsewhere. In the western North Pacific, the gray whale was so heavily hunted that it was declared extinct as recently as 1970 before a remnant population of about a hundred animals was rediscovered in the Okhotsk Sea. Bowhead whales were essentially extirpated from Spitsbergen, where once they supported a huge whaling industry led by the Dutch and the English.

Happily, many other populations of whales seem to be doing well. Humpback whales are recovering strongly in most of the areas in which they are currently studied. Likewise, western Arctic bowheads, eastern North Pacific blue whales, eastern gray whales (those that migrate along the California coast) and many populations of blue, sei and minke whales all seem to be increasing.

And not all the news about right whales is dismal. Several populations of southern right whales seem to be healthy and expanding. Among these are those off South Africa, off Argentina, and in the Auckland Islands south of New Zealand (though to date right whales have yet to reappear in significant numbers off the coast of New Zealand itself). Surveys conducted by scientists including Peter Best, Victoria Rowntree and Nathalie Patenaude have all found substantial increases in population size in these areas, and there is no reason to doubt that a similar trend is occurring among right whales from some other portions of the Southern Hemisphere.

However, for the two species living north of the equator it is a very different story. As we have seen, European right whales – medieval hunts for which initiated the long history of commercial whaling – have now disappeared entirely. Their counterparts in the western North Atlantic number perhaps 300 animals and are now largely confined to a small portion of the species' historic range, from Florida to Nova Scotia. In the eastern North Pacific, right whales cling precariously to existence following illegal Soviet catches in the 1960s; there may be at most 100 animals left alive today, and only one calf has been recorded there in over a century of observations. Finally, the western North Pacific population probably numbers in the low hundreds and may be making a slow recovery, although to date no surveys have been conducted to assess the current status of these animals. This population was also impacted by illegal hunting, in addition to centuries of unregulated coastal whaling by the Japanese.

Today there is no more hunting for right whales, but in some areas whaling has been replaced by other threats which are just as deadly. The last known intentional catch of a North Atlantic right whale was in 1935, yet despite almost seven decades of protection from hunting, this species is clearly not recovering. And once more, humans are largely responsible, albeit unintentionally. Unfortunately, the modern range of this population of some 300 whales coincides with considerable human activity, notably in the form of ship traffic and commercial fishing.

Right whales and ships are a poor mix. Unfortunately, the principal feeding and calving habitats for North Atlantic right whales are either adjacent to, or directly overlap, major shipping lanes. Because right whales are slow and spend so much time at the surface, they are particularly vulnerable to collisions with ships. Their large size

A right whale at the surface, head towards the top of the photo. Their tendency to spend a lot of time at the surface increases their vulnerability to ship collisions.

does little to buffer them from such accidents: a 10,000 ton freighter striking a 50-ton right whale can kill it instantly, and it is unlikely that the crew of the ship would even be aware of the collision.

Why whales get hit is not entirely clear. Ships are certainly very loud and there is little doubt that a whale can hear an approaching vessel from a considerable distance.

However, the problem may be one of habituation. There is so much ship traffic in many areas that if whales responded to every ship passing within even half a mile, they would be constantly reacting and would have little time for feeding or other activities. Instead, they may not respond until a ship is very close – and sometimes this may mean that they leave it too late to get out of the way of a fast-moving vessel.

This whale's tail stock clearly shows old wounds inflicted by a boat propeller.

The hydrodynamics of ships create additional problems. A whale may be struck by the bow of a ship, or if the animal is too close to the side it may be sucked in by the movement of the vessel through the water. If this happens, a whale may end up being drawn into the ship's propellers and killed. Indeed, we have seen a number of cases of whales with huge slashes down the length of their bodies, the result of a collision with the massive blades of a propeller.

This type of strike is very obvious, but others may not be, and assigning cause of death in such situations is a difficult task. Whales that die of natural causes may be struck post-mortem by a passing ship; in such cases, a necropsy will reveal no major hemorrhaging, since there is no active blood circulation in a dead body. In contrast, a whale that *was* struck when alive may exhibit no obvious external injury. This is counter-intuitive; one would think that when something the size of a ship hits a whale the damage will be obvious, but it sometimes isn't.

A good example of this occurred in April 1999, when a large and probably very old female right whale named Staccato washed up dead on a beach on Cape Cod. Staccato had first been seen in 1977 and had had at least six calves; she was a familiar whale, and had been photographed alive in Cape Cod Bay just a few days before her death.

Staccato's carcass was whole and there was no obvious indication of what had killed her. A full necropsy was conducted, and over the course of two days this 45-foot, 60-ton animal was flensed down to the bone by an expert team from the New England Aquarium and the Woods Hole Oceanographic Institution. Nothing obvious was apparent until the end of the second day, when they finally reached Staccato's right jaw. The jaw was massively fractured, and the tissue surrounding it showed major hemorrhaging. Clearly, Staccato had suffered a ship strike, and had been alive at the time. Subsequent microscopic analysis of her tissues suggested that she had remained alive for about a week after the collision before finally succumbing to her injuries.

In most cases, deaths from ship strikes are quick and probably painless. But this is not the case for the other major source of mortality in right whales and many other large whales: entanglement in fishing gear.

Every year worldwide hundreds of thousands of whales, dolphins and porpoises are killed by entanglements. Small cetaceans usually drown in nets, but large whales are frequently powerful enough to drag the fishing gear away with them after the initial entanglement. Studies of entanglement scars on right whales indicate that more than two-thirds of the entire population has been entangled at some point in their lives. This analysis also indicates that an astonishing 10-20% of all individuals become entangled in any one year.

Rope protrudes from the mouth of an entangled right whale.

Sometimes the injuries from an entanglement are minor and the whale sheds the gear, leaving telltale scars on its body. In other cases, however, the gear may be so heavy that it restricts the whale's ability to move and feed, and the animal will suffer a slow death from starvation. And sometimes the weight of gear results in rope embedding itself so deeply in the whale's flesh that it becomes a pathway to a serious infection that eventually kills the animal.

The most famous case of this involved an adult male North Atlantic right whale named Churchill. During the summer of 2000, Churchill became entangled in some unknown type of fishing gear. We will never know exactly what happened, but it is very likely that on first encountering the gear, Churchill twisted in an attempt to escape the line. In doing so, however, a loop of rope wound around the whale's narrow rostrum (the upper part of the head), and then was pulled tight – very tight – by the weight of fishing gear on either side of it. As a result, the rope became deeply embedded in Churchill's rostrum, and infection set in.

Over the course of that summer, a rescue team from the Center for Coastal Studies in Provincetown, Massachusetts made several attempts to free Churchill, but without success. One problem with right whales is that, unlike most humpback whales, they are anything but passive during such rescue attempts. The Center's standard method of pacifying an entangled whale is to attach a line to some part of the entangling gear, and then attach a series of very large plastic floats to the line. The buoyancy of these floats slows the animal down and, in the case of most humpback whales, will force it to eventually stop at the surface, where disentanglement can then be attempted.

Not so with right whales. These animals react very aggressively, thrashing their huge tails and frequently towing any boat at the end of the attachment line for miles. Disentangling a right whale is one of the most dangerous of tasks, and the people who attempt this – led by the Center's Charles Mayo and David Mattila – are quite literally risking their lives to do so.

Because of this danger, and after several frightening interactions with Churchill, the Center wisely decided that no further attempts would be made unless the whale could somehow be sedated. At that point, however, no one had ever attempted to sedate a free-swimming whale. The problems involved were immense. First, whales are voluntary breathers and as a result they cannot be anesthetized or they will 'forget' to breathe and die. Second, an animal the size of a right whale requires a huge dose of any sedative, and delivering this dose into the animal's body was an equally massive challenge. Next, no one knew what dose to give: too little, and there would be no effect; too much, and they risked harming or even killing the whale.

A team of veterinarians decided to use a mild sedative, and calculated a conservative dose to be used on Churchill. Meanwhile, Michael Moore and a team of

The great triangular tail of one whale is raised high in the air
as a group of right whales all arch their backs and dive.

very creative engineers from the Woods Hole Oceanographic Institution designed a spring-loaded, three-prong system which could rapidly deliver the drug into the whale's tissue.

The delivery system worked remarkably well on the first attempt, but it was clear that the dose of the sedative was too small. Subsequent attempts involved higher dosages, and on the third attempt the whale did indeed appear to become quieter and more relaxed. Sadly, however, the embedded line could neither be removed nor cut, and it was clear with each sighting of Churchill that his health was seriously deteriorating. Finally, in the autumn the satellite transmitter that had been attached with a tether to the whale suddenly stopped sending signals, and there is little doubt that this reflected the death of this individual. Churchill died in deep water offshore, and was so emaciated from months of starvation that his carcass likely sank, never to be recovered.

Much had been learned from this experience about how to deal with an entangled right whale, but ultimately the whale itself could not be saved. Some other disentanglements have been successful, but the ratio of rescues to entanglements remains low.

Together, ship collisions and fishing gear entanglements probably kill several right whales a year, and this continuing human-caused mortality has kept the North Atlantic population from recovering. In fact, the situation is perhaps worse than a failure to recover: recent demographic analyses by several biologists have indicated that the population is probably declining.

To make matters worse, there is some evidence that North Atlantic right whales may suffer from reproductive dysfunction: the number of calves born each year varies wildly, from as few as one to more than 30, and the overall reproductive rate is about half that of the southern right whale. Various explanations have been advanced for this phenomenon, including inbreeding, pollution, disease and nutritional stress. Of these, the only one for which there is some evidence is the latter: the idea that reproduction is affected by food availability. The body condition of right whales — essentially, how fat they are — seems to be correlated with the annual abundance of their planktonic prey. Since a lean female is less able to support the huge cost of lactation, it is not unlikely that body condition has a direct impact on a whale's ability to bear and successfully raise a calf.

The southern right whale population seems to have none of these problems, and is growing rapidly. The North Pacific right whale is known to be affected by entanglements, although the extent to which this is a problem is unclear. However, with so few right whales remaining in both the North Pacific and North Atlantic, any unnatural mortality is one mortality too many.

Solutions to the problems of ship collisions and entanglements are not easy to craft, but attempts are being made, notably in the North Atlantic. Although some interim measures have recently been enacted to attempt to reduce the frequency of right whale entanglements, most biologists believe that the only long-term solution to this problem will come from modification of fishing gear. In other words, we need to design future fishing gear so that whales are less likely to be become entangled and fishermen can continue to fish. Whether this is indeed a practicable undertaking is not clear, but gear modification has now become a major priority for research and development work.

On the ship strike issue, the governments of both the United States and Canada are working to develop measures to reduce the likelihood that right whales and ships will collide. Recently, the shipping lanes in the Bay of Fundy — the major known summer habitat for this species — were moved away from the major concentrations of feeding right whales. This was no small accomplishment given the

Many right whale habitats are close to shipping lanes. The increase in ship traffic, and trend towards faster vessels, pose increasing threats for right whales.

complexities of international maritime law and the many logistical challenges involved, and it was due to concerted efforts by Moira Brown, Lindy Johnson and a number of Canadian officials. Other regulations are being considered to reroute or slow down shipping in key areas for right whales along the east coast of the United States.

At this point, we do not know whether these various measures will prove successful in the conservation of right whales. But while complete success may be desirable, it is not essential for the short-term: recent research suggests that reducing anthropogenic mortalities by even two or three individuals (notably mature females) per year may reverse the decline of the North Atlantic right whale.

The future for right whales, then, remains uncertain. While southern rights continue to prosper, the continued existence of their Northern Hemisphere counterparts is by no means assured. No longer threatened by hunting, right whales in both the North Atlantic and North Pacific have a long uphill road to recovery in the face of new dangers from shipping, fishing gear, habitat degradation and perhaps pollution. Both northern species may also suffer from inbreeding and other problems that arise whenever a population is reduced to low numbers.

With the possible exception of the Atlantic gray whale – which became extinct around 1800 for reasons that remain unclear – and despite the relentless greed of the whaling industry, humans have yet to cause the extinction of a species of large whale. But in the two species of northern right whales we have come perilously close.

Recently, whenever I have seen right whales in the field, I have found myself entertaining the sad thought that mine may be among the last generations of people to see this strange and remarkable animal plying the waters of the North Atlantic and North Pacific Oceans. I very much hope that I am wrong.

Right Whale Distribution

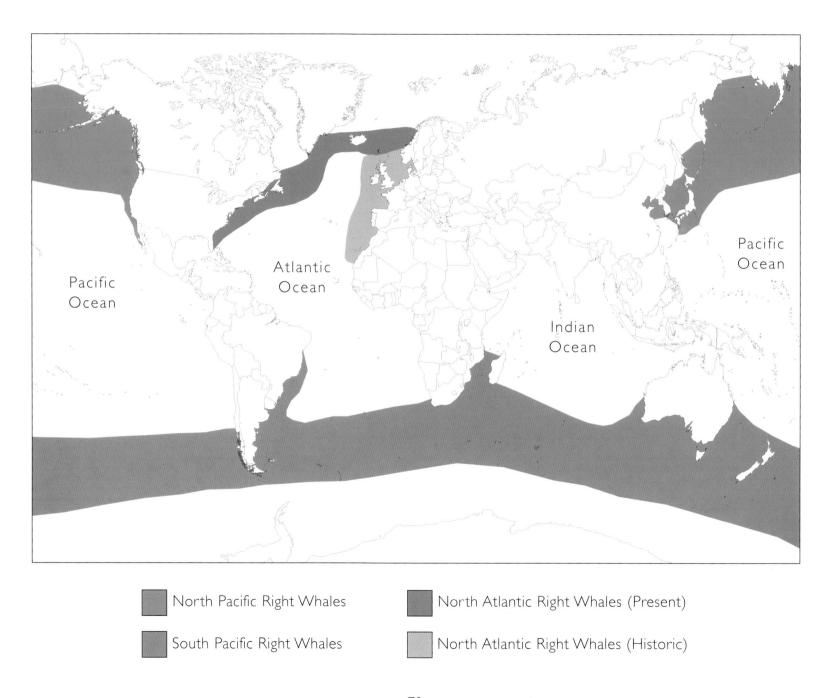

Pacific Ocean

Atlantic Ocean

Indian Ocean

Pacific Ocean

North Pacific Right Whales

South Pacific Right Whales

North Atlantic Right Whales (Present)

North Atlantic Right Whales (Historic)

Right Whale Facts

Scientific name:	*Eubalaena glacialis*	(North Atlantic right whale)
	Eubalaena japonica	(North Pacific right whale)
	Eubalaena australis	(Southern right whale)
Average length	(adult female):	46 feet (14 meters)
	(adult male):	43 feet (13 meters)
	(newborn calf):	14 feet (4.3 meters)
Average adult weight	(female):	40-50 tons
Maximum weight	(female):	100 tons
Maximum breadth of tail:		20 feet (6 meters)
Longevity:		At least 70 years

Reproduction – Both males and females are sexually mature at an average age of about 7-9 years. The gestation period is approximately 11.5 months. Females give birth to a single calf, on average every three or four years. Calves usually leave their mothers towards the end of their natal year.

Distribution – Right whales are found in the North Atlantic, the North Pacific and throughout much of the Southern Hemisphere, in both coastal and offshore habitats. They feed in high-latitude waters in spring, summer and autumn, and some whales (notably pregnant females) migrate to warmer waters to calve in winter. The whereabouts of much of any right whale population in winter remains unknown.

Recommended Reading

Whales by Phil Clapham, Colin Baxter, 1997. A beautifully illustrated overview of all the world's large whales.
The Audubon Guide to Marine Mammals by Randall Reeves, Brent Stewart, Phil Clapham and James Powell, Knopf, New York, 2002. A thoroughly researched and up to date field guide to all marine mammals.
Men and Whales by Richard Ellis, Knopf, New York, 1991. An outstanding popular account of the history of whaling.

Index

archaeocetes 12, 13
Argentina 25, 46, 57
Auckland Islands 23, 57
Australia 23, 41
baleen 8, 13, 17, 18, 20, 21, 30, 33, 34, 35, 37, 38, 41, 42, 52
Basques 49, 50
Bay of Fundy 26, 66
behavior 26, 30, 36, 37, 41, 43, 46, 51
Best, Peter 57
birth 11, 41, 43
blubber 8, 18, 34, 50
breaching 13, 27, 46
Brown, Moira 30, 68
Brownell, Bob 25, 54
callosities 17, 18, 19, 21, 25, 35
calves 41, 42, 43, 50, 61, 65, 71
calving 22, 41, 42, 52, 58
Cape Cod 8, 29, 61
cetaceans 11, 12, 13, 21, 61
Cintra Bay 41, 52
classification and evolution 12-14
condylarths 12
Conger, Lisa 27
conservation 8, 57, 68
copepods 33, 34, 38
cyamids (whale lice) 18
disease 66
entanglement 8, 61, 62, 63, 65, 66
evolution 12, 14, 17, 30
feeding 8, 20, 26, 33, 34, 35, 37, 38, 42, 58, 60, 66
flippers 12, 14, 21, 23, 44
Florida 22, 29, 41, 58

genetic analysis 12, 14, 30
  studies 13
gestation 42, 71
Hamilton, Philip 27
head 7, 12, 17, 18, 19, 30, 32, 35, 51, 58, 62
identification 19, 25, 30
inbreeding 30, 66, 68
International Whaling Commission 53, 57
Johnson, Lindy 2, 68
Knowlton, Amy 27
Kraus, Scott 2
Labrador 30, 51
lactation 42, 66
Marx, Marilyn 27, 29
mating 8, 43, 44, 45, 46
Mattila, David 63
Mayflower 7
Mayo, Charles 34, 63
milk 11, 41
Moore, Michael 63
mouth 13, 18, 20, 21, 34, 38, 41, 42, 62
mysticetes 13, 37
New England 8, 51, 61
New England Aquarium 26, 27, 29, 61
New Zealand 23, 57
nursing 41, 42
odontocetes 13
Okhotsk Sea 22, 53, 57
Patenaude, Nathalie 23, 57
Payne, Roger 25, 46
Pilgrims 7, 8, 51
pollution 66, 68
population 22, 23, 25, 26, 27, 30, 52, 53, 54, 58, 62, 65, 66, 68, 71

population size 57
pregnancy 41, 46
prey 13, 33, 35, 37, 38, 42, 50, 66
range 22, 23, 26, 51, 58
reproduction 17, 41, 66, 71
rescue 63, 65
right whales, appearance 17
  classification 13, 14
  evolution 12, 13, 14, 17, 30
  North Atlantic 8, 14, 21, 22, 26, 27, 29, 30, 41, 51, 52, 58, 62, 65, 66, 68, 71
  North Pacific 8, 14, 17, 21, 41, 53, 54, 58, 66, 68, 71
  present status 54, 58
  range, historic 22, 23, 51, 58
    present 23, 26
  size and weight 17, 18, 41, 44, 45, 54, 58, 63
  southern 14, 17, 21, 22, 23, 25, 41, 46, 51, 54, 57, 65, 66, 68, 71
Rosenbaum, Howard 14, 30
Rowntree, Victoria 57
'sailing' 36, 46
ship collisions 8, 58, 60, 61, 65, 66
South Africa 41, 57
Soviet Union 54
tail 7, 12, 17, 21, 32, 36, 41, 60, 64, 71
testes 44, 45
tongue 21, 49
whale lice 18
whaling 22, 23, 25, 27, 30, 41, 49, 50, 51, 53, 54, 57, 58, 68
White, Brad 30
zooplankton 33, 35, 37

Biographical Note

Phil Clapham has worked with large whales since 1980. He currently directs a whale research program in Woods Hole, Massachusetts, and is a Research Associate with the Smithsonian Institution in Washington DC. Cornish by birth, Clapham holds a PhD in zoology from the University of Aberdeen. He has published several other books and about a hundred scientific papers on whale biology and conservation.